A MACDONALD BOOK

Text copyright © Margaret Linton and Trevor Terry 1989
Illustrations copyright © Tricia Newell 1989

First published in Great Britain in 1989
by Macdonald & Company (Publishers) Ltd
London & Sydney
A member of Maxwell Pergamon Publishing Corporation plc.

Printed and bound in Great Britain by
Purnell Book Production Ltd
A member of BPCC plc

Main text set in 16pt Bembo Educational by Goodfellow & Egan Ltd

Macdonald & Co (Publishers) Ltd
66-73 Shoe Lane
London EC4P 4AB

British Library Cataloguing in Publication Data
Linton, Margaret, *1927* –
    Busy woodmouse.
    I. Title   II. Terry, Trevor   III. Series
    599.32'33

ISBN 0–356–13888–7
ISBN 0–356–13889–5 Pbk

• NATURE TALES •

·BUSY WOODMOUSE·

Written by Margaret Linton and Trevor Terry
Illustrated by Tricia Newell

Macdonald

It was an Autumn afternoon, and over
in Big Wood everything was still and quiet.

Woodmouse, whose warm and cosy nest
was in a tunnel under the ground, was
curled up with her babies.

Like all woodmice, she slept for most of
the day, but at night she was busy looking
for things to eat.

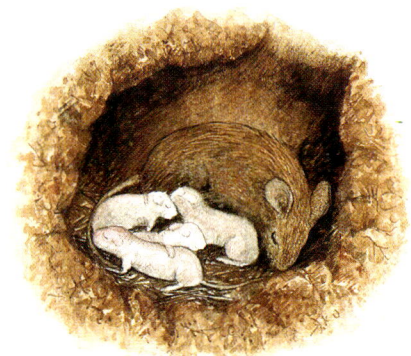

Woodmouse lived with lots of other mice, and they had nests and babies too. Their tunnels joined hers, and it was like one big family, all living together.

In some tunnels there were store rooms. Here the mice kept the seeds and berries which they were busy collecting for the Winter.

Digging tunnels and collecting food was hard work for tiny woodmice.

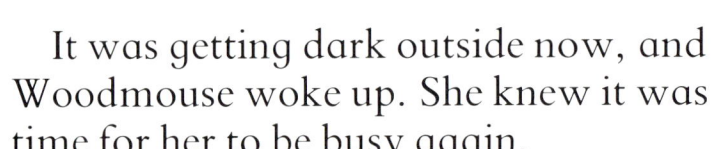

It was getting dark outside now, and Woodmouse woke up. She knew it was time for her to be busy again.

Leaving her babies fast asleep, she went to the end of one of the tunnels and began to make a new store room. She scratched at the soil and bit through roots which got in her way.

Soon it was finished and off she went to look for food.

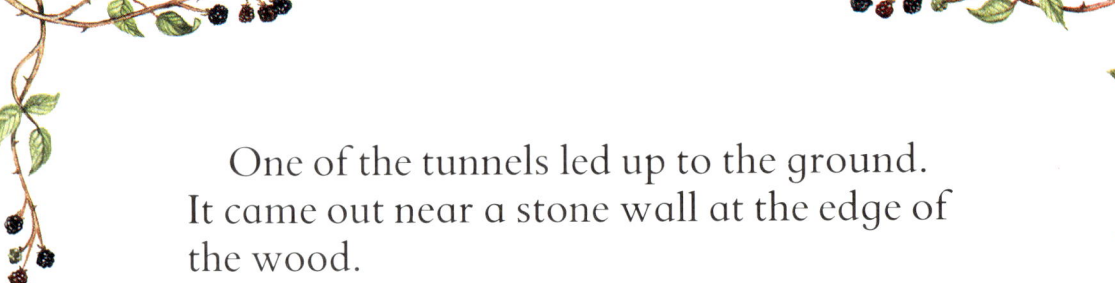

One of the tunnels led up to the ground.
It came out near a stone wall at the edge of
the wood.

Woodmouse poked her head out of the
hole and looked around. It was a clear
night, and the moon was shining brightly.

She twitched her whiskers and sniffed
the air. It felt safe to go, so out she popped.

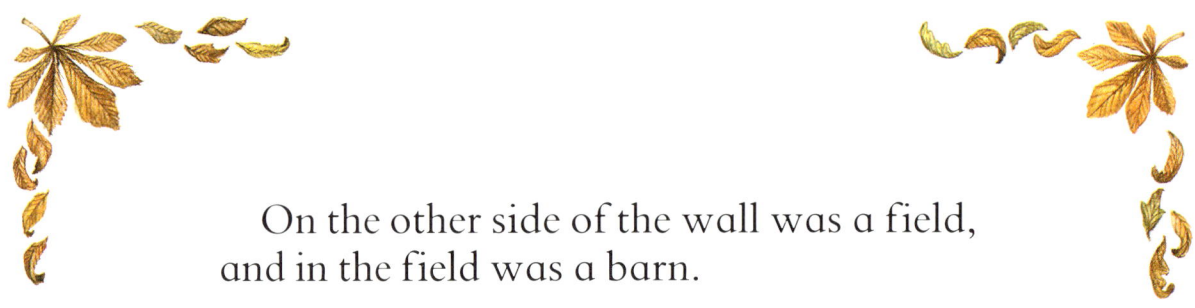

On the other side of the wall was a field, and in the field was a barn.

"That's where I'll go," said Woodmouse. She jumped through a hole in the wall and skipped along a path which the mice had made in the grass. Her big bright eyes helped her to see clearly, and her big ears could hear the slightest sound.

The barn door was shut, but Woodmouse squeezed under it and ran across to some sacks of corn. She nibbled a hole in one, and filled her mouth with corn seeds.

"I'll take these to my store room," she thought, "and then I'll come back for some more."

Backwards and forwards she ran, and the little pile of seeds in her store room grew bigger and bigger.

Woodmouse looked at the pile of seeds. "Just once more," she thought, and off she went – along the tunnels, out of the hole, through the wall and along the path to the barn.

She filled her mouth with seeds and ran back along the path. Suddenly she stopped. Standing in front of her was Weasel who had been hiding in the hole in the wall.

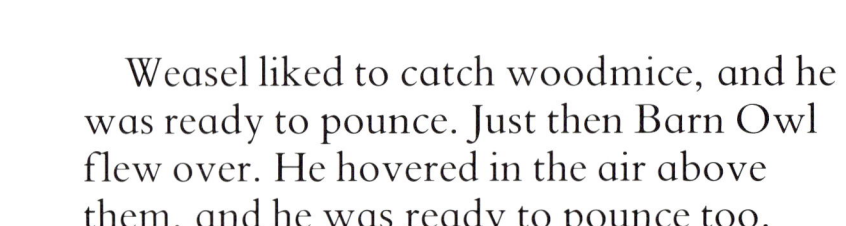

Weasel liked to catch woodmice, and he was ready to pounce. Just then Barn Owl flew over. He hovered in the air above them, and he was ready to pounce too.

Weasel looked up at Barn Owl and Barn Owl looked down at Weasel. For a moment they both forgot to look at Woodmouse.

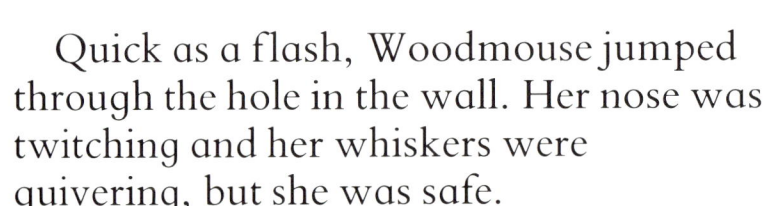

Quick as a flash, Woodmouse jumped
through the hole in the wall. Her nose was
twitching and her whiskers were
quivering, but she was safe.

"That was an exciting end to my busy
night," she thought. "Thank goodness they
didn't catch me!" And she ran back down
the tunnels to her nest and her babies.

toadstools

hips

moss

conkers

hazel nuts

pheasant

blackberries

squirrel

sweet chestnuts

haws

Autumn leaves

bat